D1827806

Letters to Madiba

voices of South African children

This book is dedicated to all the children of South Africa

We are grateful for and inspired by your hope, your courage and your positive spirit in building a truly equal, just and vibrant South Africa.

Foreword

Political analysts, editors, politicians, world leaders, sports and cultural spokespersons – representatives of every stratum of society have made pronouncements on Nelson Mandela. Now at long last the children of South Africa are having their say to their favourite grandfather.

This book is undoubtedly a very important landmark in the long history of the symbiotic relationship between Madiba and the children, characterised by mutually deep and overwhelming love.

When we were prisoners on Robben Island, I wrote in a letter, after a visit from a child, 'I shall always remember how I returned to the cell that day with my mind in a whirl. It was the first time in 20 years that I had come in such close physical contact with a child; I actually held her and kissed her.' Until that point, '… our world has been without children, an unreal world. One needs a child's approach to things: openness, generosity, total absence of selfishness, no sense of property, no respect for adult red tape, a scorn for unrighteousness and injustice, a happy, carefree, loving attitude. Every visit from a child brings to us a breath of fresh air …'

It is true that children may not understand complex philosophical, political or cultural concepts. However, call it instinct if you like, but the natural and spontaneously innocent responses of children even to complex concepts cannot be faulted. They are uninhibited, frank and honest.

The letters, poems and drawings in this book encapsulate, very simply and powerfully, the innermost feelings of children – their appreciation and affection for their beloved Madiba, and their fears, their ambitions and their wishes. Their work is brimming with the spirit of hope and optimism and great pride in who they are and in their country, South Africa. At the same time they sensitively raise concerns about our country's biggest problems and challenges.

Above all, they highlight a heart-rending cry to be acknowledged and to be taken seriously, to be heard.

As a country, as Government, as a nation – we dare not ignore the pleas coming from the little hearts of our most-prized citizens, the children. Together, let us put the 'child' back into 'childhood'.

Am Kathrada

Ahmed Kathrada
17 December 2001
Chairperson of the Robben Island Museum Council
Former Political Prisoner
Former Member of Parliament and Parliamentary Counsellor
in the Office of President Mandela

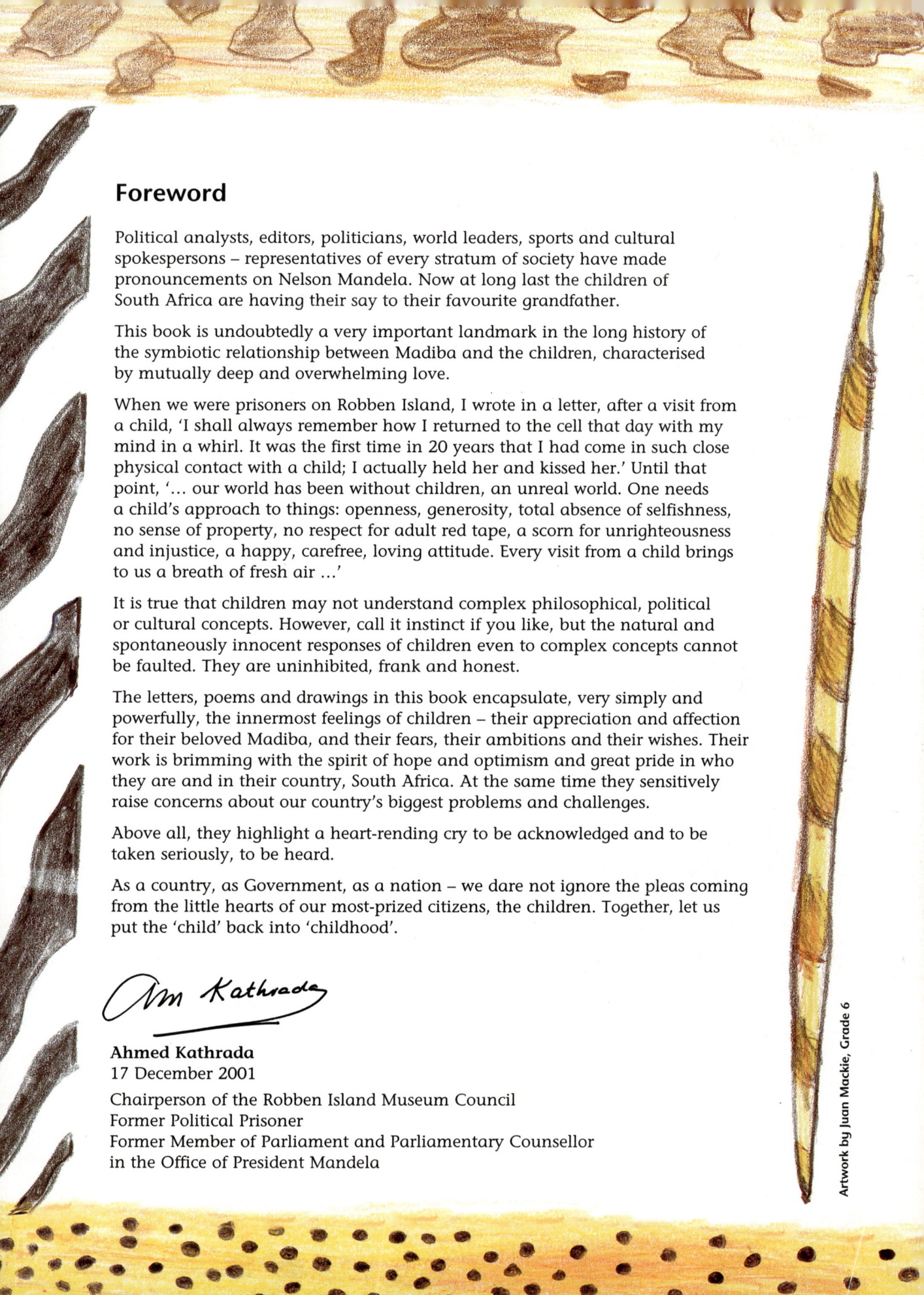

Artwork by Juan Mackie, Grade 6

Artwork by Trevona

Introduction

When we asked children to write to Nelson Mandela to tell him why they are proud to be South African, over 800 000 children seized the opportunity to communicate their feelings. This inspiring collection represents a selection of the very best entries.

The competition was a joint venture of Simba and Maskew Miller Longman. Inspired by the fact that 2001 was *The Year of the Reader* in South Africa, Simba commissioned Hotdogz Inc. to develop a programme to celebrate the magic power of books and their ability to educate and inform our children. During 2001 the Simba road show visited children in thousands of primary schools across the country and invited them to participate in the *Letters to Madiba* challenge.

Seven judges, whose names appear below, chose this compilation of writing and artwork. It is a celebration of life in South Africa. The work is creative, spontaneous, honest and humorous. It shows children at their best. It is also a tribute to their parents and teachers, whose wisdom has nurtured the spirit of reconciliation and the knowledge of South Africa's painful and triumphant history, that characterise so many of the entries.

At Maskew Miller Longman we have edited the writing carefully. We have kept the children's own words and removed only glaring spelling and grammatical errors. The authorship of each piece of work has been acknowledged where it was supplied to us. Not all pieces were entered with details of their origins. If you recognise a letter or drawing, please contact us, so that the correct details can be included in future editions.

The publisher

Panel of judges for the *Letters to Madiba* competition

Mandla Maseko, Campaign Manager, Masifunde Sonke, National Department of Education

Lisa Blakeway, Editor, ReadRight, *Sunday Times*

Edwin Naidu, Editor, *The Teacher*

Ted Lineham, Marketing Director, Simba

Jeremy Boraine, Marketing Manager, Maskew Miller Longman

Rosemary Cohen, ReadRight, Distribution and Teacher Training Co-ordinator

Janis Chapman, Donor Relations Manager, Nelson Mandela Children's Fund

I am happy because I love the way I look and who I am

Khayelitsha
Cape Town

26 September 2001

Dear Madiba

Thank you for everything that you've done for South Africa. I am in a school because of you. I am happy because I love the way I look and who I am. I am a South African girl and I am happy inside.

I am also happy to write this letter because I never thought that there would be a thing like this: writing a letter to Madiba. I go to a primary school in Cape Town and I'm proud to be in this school because I learn lots of interesting things especially maths. I love maths.

I would love it if you would visit our school one day. Madiba, I hope you will live a happy life till the end of your world.

Yours faithfully

Aphelile Makubalo

Artwork by Sadiya Manuel, Grade 5

5

I wish that I could destroy this killing virus called Aids

Kwazakhele
Port Elizabeth

Dear Mr Mandela

I'm writing this to thank you for being a South African hero. I'm not old enough to know the whole story about your past, but I am impressed with what I've heard.

I am happy that I was born in this country. There are many things to be proud about. I want to grow up in peace in my motherland. I am aiming to be my world's pride and hope. I want to help other people as much as I can. I wish that I could destroy this killing virus called Aids. I pray that I grow up before it hurts many people so that I can save those souls by discovering the cure.

I believe that all my dreams will come true and I will be a hero of my country one day. I know that will happen soon although I am only eleven years old now.

Thank you

Zimasa Makaula (a proud little South African)

(Age 11)

Artwork by Taariq

Eldorado Park

Dear Madiba

I am not only proud but also very ecstatic to be a South African.

This wonderful country of ours has so many things to offer due to our diverse cultures and unity made possible by our culture of ubuntu.

There is no other place in the world I would rather be since we live on a continent that can boast with flora and fauna not found on other continents.

As if that is not enough, the Nkosi has blessed us with wonderful weather for this rainbow nation to grow stronger in this African Renaissance for a better future.

We love you and siyabonga Madiba.

Nkosi sikelel' iAfrika

Loréal Ryan

(Grade 5)

Artwork by Roxanne Snyman, 8 years

8

Dear Madiba

I'm writing this letter to tell you how much I enjoy being a South African child. Before I talk further let me introduce myself. My name is Thembeka and my surname is Ndlela. I am a 13-year-old Zulu speaking girl. I go to Bree Primary School in Mayfair West 7th Avenue. I live in town at Hillbrow. I live with my mother and my brothers and sisters.

Now I can go further with my talking. I'm proud to be a South African child because people of South Africa like working as a nation. When I was young I didn't know anything about what was going on around me, but as the years went by I started knowing what kind of a country South Africa was. As I grew up I used to hear words like rapist and thief. I didn't know what these words meant until I came to this school in 1994 and they explained to us what rapists and thieves are. So people of South Africa are trying to catch all these criminals by all means. All kinds of organisations are working to make this country crime-free. I wish that God never brought these thieves to our country.

I would like to sit and talk, but I gotta go!

See you whenever we meet, and I just hope my letter gets to you.

Bye!

Thembeka Ndlela

(Age 13)

You could bring your wife too; she would get on well with my mom

Artwork by Katy

Dear Madiba

I have been thinking about why we are proud to be South African children. One thing I'm really proud about, is that we have you as our father and our leader. We have you to look up to and to love. You have shown us that through love and respect and loyalty we can grow up to be the kind of person that you are. You didn't have the easy, cosy life that I have, but yet, look at how you turned out! I would be proud to even just be one grey hair on your famous head!!!!!!!!!!!!!!!!!!

I am proud to be a South African child, because my parents have taught me to love and respect people for who they are. When I look at people, I don't see colour, I see happy faces or good friends. It makes life so much easier when you are comfortable with people who are Xhosa or Indian or Zulu.

I am proud of our beautiful country. Cape Town is the best! I would love it if you came for lunch with me in Noordhoek. I would take you to Kim's farmstall for lunch. We could sit on the stoep. You would really love the view of Chapman's Peak. My brother could take you on the four-wheeler to the lookout point and you could see the whole of the Fish Hoek valley and Noordhoek beach, and Kommetjie. You could bring your wife too; she would get on well with my mom.

I am proud to be me, and I am working hard at school to learn everything I can, so when I am big I can follow in your footsteps and do great things and make a difference to all of us in South Africa.

Last year, when I was in Grade 3, I wrote an essay about what I would do if I was president of this country. This is what I wrote:

> If I were president I would always try to be good and kind and caring so that I would be a good example for others. I will stop all TV from 7 p.m. to 9 p.m. so families can have time to talk or argue with each other and fix problems. All children would learn to read and write and learn cooking so they could help in the house. Children would learn to look after their pets and to deworm their dogs and cats.
>
> I would teach families to care for their grannies and grandpas at home and not just dump them in horrid old age homes where they get smacked. All children who are naughty at school would have to work at the police station and do jobs like cleaning the toilets, sweeping the cells and killing the fleas and lice on the blankets. They would do this every day after school. THEN they would be good. All children would have good manners. If they were rude, they would wear T-shirts for one week that say "I AM RUDE". All families would have to learn about recycling and everyone would have a turn to sweep the pavements and pick up litter. If you didn't wear a seatbelt, you would be banned from driving a car. And there would be NO drinking and driving in my country. Everyone would get a free lunch on Sunday, if they went to church first. And they would have to pray they could be good all week till the next free lunch.
>
> If someone built a house for the poor they would get free petrol for one month and extra house points for their house at school.

That is the end of my essay and I hope you have found it interesting. You can see that I plan to do great things one day.

Thank you for making me proud to be who I am.

With lots of love

Dani van Zyl

(Grade 4)

Artwork by Katy

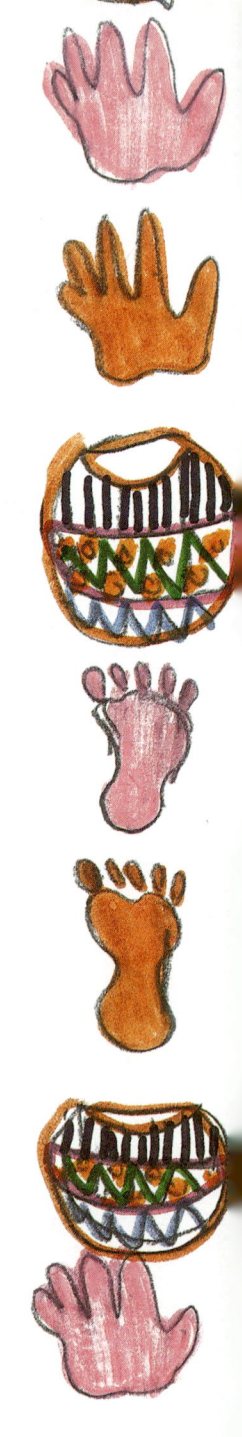

Dear Mr Mandela

I have written you a story that I hope will make you understand why I am proud to be a child of Africa.

Anyone would be proud of their nation if it had overcome racism, apartheid and many other problems, like we have. Although we still suffer from problems like poverty and crime there are many more good aspects than there are bad, and to me that is a great accomplishment.

We call Africa the rainbow nation because there are so many different races in Africa. I believe that the only thing separating us is our belief that because we have different colour skins or different religions we are different to other people.

Africa is a beautiful country with wonderful people in it as well as magical places left untouched, where the wild animals run freely. In the hot days when the sun beats down on Africa, the ferocious lions sleep under the trees, while the elephants cool down in the river. Where the animals live there are beautiful sunsets that instantly become special moments the minute you watch them.

So now you've heard my story, which tells why I'm proud, proud to be a child of Africa. I hope that anyone who reads this will also be proud to belong to Mother Africa.

Tansy Bensusann
(Grade 5)

Artwork by Tansy Bensusann, Grade 5

I go to bed with a smile on my face and wake up with hope in my heart that South Africa will be like Disneyland to all its children.

Dear Madiba

My name is Keabetswe Seate. I am 10 years old and I have a twelve-year-old brother. I live in North Cliff Extension 25 and I go to Cliff View Primary School in Johannesburg, Gauteng.

I am proud to be a South African because you taught me the difference between right and wrong and between pain and joy. You taught me the difference between love and hate and between having friends and being lonely. Most of all you have given me the power of choice to choose what is best for me. You have given me the chance to dream and to build castles in the air and to imagine a better world for children.

I go to bed with a smile on my face and wake up with hope in my heart that South Africa will be like Disneyland to all its children.

Your loving grandchild

Keabetswe Seate

(Age 10)

Thank you Madiba
I love you

Artwork by Lerato Mbhele, Grade 7

13

Dear Madiba

I would like to thank you for your great contribution and sacrifice you have made for our country. I sometimes think of all the years you spent on Robben Island away from your family and friends. Was it very lonely?

I am nine years old.

My greatest wish is to meet you face to face. We would sit together and talk about all your adventures. I know I would learn many things from you. Your family and friends must be so happy to have you back again.

Yours faithfully

Nakeeta

(Age 9)

I wish you a long and happy life.

Artwork by Sheldon Izaakse, Grade 1

14

Artwork by Doughie Machubeni, Grade 3

Different faces
Many races
Different people
Many places
The past behind us
The future and freedom in front of us

For children of Africa
We stand together
Through violence and racism
We stand together
In these troubled times
We stand together

We come from one land but we are so different
Yet, we stand together.

Stephen-John Martin

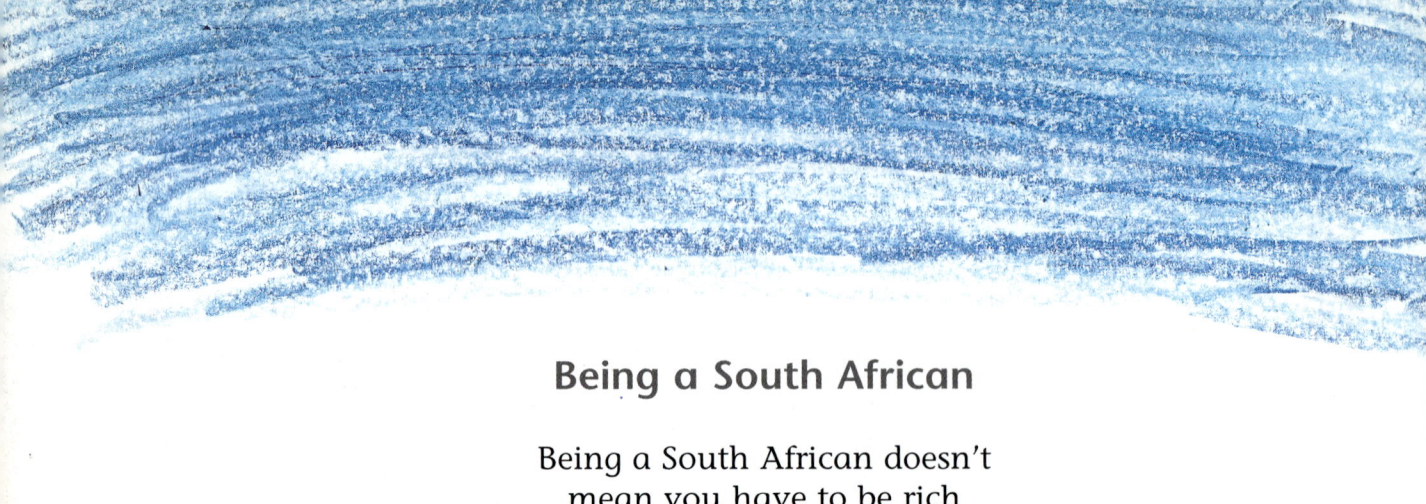

Being a South African

Being a South African doesn't
mean you have to be rich
it doesn't mean you have to be poor
it doesn't mean you have to show off.
it means to know your culture
to live with people and know who you are.

How proud I am

I am proud of my culture
I'm proud of my country
I'm proud of myself
I'm proud of you Mr Nelson Mandela
For bringing us to freedom
And bringing us peace in
Our LAND
We thank you very much.

Lesedi Sebuetseba

Artwork by Athenkosi Jacobs, 7 years

Kommetjie

22 October 2001

Dear Madiba

My name is Justice, I go to Kommetjie Primary. (I arrived only a few days ago – so far so good!) I am writing this letter to say how proud I am to be a South African child.

I am proud to be a South African because our race is mixed and we come from a new generation of young South Africans. I was born in the year you were released! Since then you have been my role model because you were not angry and didn't hate the people who caused you harm.

I have only three wishes – my first one is that apartheid never happened so our adults would tolerate each other much more.

My second is that there would be lots more people like you.

My third is that our nation will stay like this!

Thank you very much Madiba.

Best wishes

Justice Hoare

(Grade 5)

Artwork by Chanadia Stigling, 11 years

17

Artwork by Simone Govender, Grade 4

Letter and artwork by Nkosingiphile Tobias Ngobese, Grade 1

Now we have something we can play on

New Brighton
Port Elizabeth

11 September 2001

Dear Nelson Mandela

I write this letter to tell you how proud I am to be a child of this country.

My name is Mandisa Mate and I live in Port Elizabeth. I am happy to be one of the children who enjoys the life that you make easy for us in the township. I am very thankful for the parks that you built for us in our township. We didn't have facilities at our playground. Now we have something we can play on.

To finish my letter I just want to say you are one out of many people, who can give to the poor. You made the Nelson Mandela Children's Fund to help disabled and poor children.

Thank you so much for making this South Africa of ours a better place to be.

Yours sincerely

Mandisa Mate

(Grade 6)

Artwork by Nicholas Andrew Edmonds

We have too much HIV/Aids

To Mr Mandela

I know this letter is only for the South Africans but to speak the truth I am not a South African. But, I am proud to still stay in South Africa because it is a very lovely country to live in.

The only thing is we have too much HIV/Aids. But I know in my heart that one day all this will go away.

Sometimes I sit and just think of you. But sometimes I sit and think of what is going to happen to South Africa. But I think I know that nothing bad is going to happen.

I hope all our dreams come true. What has happened to America could happen here too. So let's just keep our country safe. I am so happy to stay in South Africa so let's pray to God and everything is going to be OK.

Sithalima

Artwork by Christelle, Grade 1

You taught me that it is more important to talk than to fight or to kill

Dube

18 June 2001

Dear Madiba

I feel so honoured to be living in the same country as you. You made me proud of my country and myself. Since you were released from prison you have brought about lots of changes. I have learned that it is very important to reconcile with someone even if the person has treated you badly. You taught me that it is more important to talk than to fight or to kill. You made me realise that my life is precious, that no one has the right to abuse me. I have rights. I have learned that I have a right to live.

You have turned South Africa into a democratic country and a rainbow nation. It is because of you that there is a children's fund to help the needy. You are the beauty of South Africa. I love you so much Madiba.

I love you Madiba.

Ofentse Makhubu

(Grade 3)

The crime rate in South Africa is very high.

Rondebosch East
Cape Town

24 October 2001

Dear Mr Mandela

I am really honoured to be a South African child because, with your help we have overcome the trauma of the apartheid era. Even though we are not a first world country we still have good resources. Our famous mountain attracts tourists from all over the world.

The crime rate in South Africa is very high. In every edition of the Cape Times I read about violence but I still don't give up on our country. We have unique vegetation and the most beautiful beaches. Our government tries very hard to maintain these resources, but other people aren't that keen. Many children would like to go to America and the UK (those are the only two countries they talk about). They don't see the true beauty of our country and don't realise what an honour it is to be a South African child.

I'm not going to change their minds overnight, but with your help we could accomplish our mission of getting everyone thinking that our country is a beautiful country and that we stand united and face our problems head-on as a nation.

Yours sincerely

Kyle Hendricks

(Grade 6)

Artwork by Shepherd Dube, Grade 7

23

South Africa

Oh! South Africa
What a beautiful country
the rivers and the sky are blue
the fields are green
and the sun is yellow

Oh! South Africa
the different beliefs and religions
the different languages and cultures
which make us a rainbow nation

Madiba ho! Madiba
If you were not there
this wonderful world would
not be here.

Kefiloe Maabane
(Grade 6)

Artwork by Kefiloe Maabane, Grade 6

24

Dear Mr Nelson Rolihlahla Mandela

I am writing this letter to you just to let you now how grateful I am for what you did for this country and how I am so glad and proud to be a South African citizen.

At school we had to imitate people and the teacher would let each one draw a person's name out of a box. So when I got my turn I had to imitate you. At first I thought it was just a fun act but now I realise it was a privilege and an honour to be you for just a second.

I thank you again for being such a great influence, not just on me but on every single South African and for being a role model that we all can look up to.

Sincerely yours

Yethu Celiwe Mhlongo

(Grade 6)

Sidwell
Port Elizabeth

14 September 2001

Dear Mr Mandela

I wish you could live many many years to come. Don't be sick again.

When you give out presents do not forget our school please. We need a computer and a library at our school. My school uniform is maroon and white. Could you give us a soccer kit and a soccer ball?

I like you when you smile Tata.

Yours faithfully

Ntsimango Zwethu

We are newsmakers, shakers and fighters for peace

Why I'm proud to be South African

To be South African makes me proud
We are one colourful nation; we stand out in a crowd.
South Africans are famous worldwide, our names always ringing
From Nobel Prizes to Olympic races and rhythmic singing.

There's Nelson Mandela, a man we all know.
And Miriam Makeba, a woman of show.
There's the colourful Bishop Tutu, known worldwide
For his outspoken manners and his strong, black pride.

This makes me proud as proud as can be.
To be a South African, we're famous you see
We are newsmakers, shakers and fighters for peace
Our pride and our patriotism should never cease.

Gabriela Brandaõ
(Grade 6)

Artwork by Gabriela Brandaõ, Grade 6

Dear Nelson Mandela
Lots of people
need food for
growing healthy
Make sure that
homes are builtsafely

I Love South Africa

Letter-writer and artist unknown, Grade 1

DEAR MR. MANDELA,

I LIKE CRICKET.   HOW DO YOU LIKE IT TO BE A SOUTH AFRICAN?

FROM JUSTIN STUART KOK

THIS I ☒ DId Bi myself

Artwork by Christine, Grade 3

PS Even though I'm white, I think apartheid
was a terrible thing.

To Mr Nelson Mandela

Stand tall with pride

There is a man named Nelson Mandela.
He will always be the best president ever.
He stands tall with pride.
He's absolutely not shy.
The white government wanted him out of the way.
But Nelson Mandela would not go away.
He was put in prison.
To die and go rotten.
His family and comrades shed many tears.
But he was let go after many years.
The African Society came to Nelson's aid.
When they all fought together against apartheid.
They fought and fought until the battle was won.
His family, his comrades, his people behind him.
Everyone in South Africa became an equal resident.
And Nelson Mandela, he became president.

Now you know why I'm proud to be a South African.

Stephen Austin
(Grade 6)

PS Even though I'm white, I think apartheid was a terrible thing.

Artwork by Andisiwe, Grade 4

Montford
Chatsworth

13 November 200

A greeting to you dear Nelson Mandela

I would like to say hello to you and congratulate you on what you have done for South Africa.

You are a very kind, humble and a polite person. Every time you were in Durban or at the Chatsworth Stadium I was very anxiously waiting to meet you but unfortunately I could not.

I admire the way you dress because you are very neat. When I see you on television I feel so proud. For your age you are a very strong and healthy person. I will like to know more about you. You did so much for South Africa and I do not know how to thank you.

I hope you like my letter. I also hope you can send me a photograph of you.

Here is a poem to you.

A man of words and of deeds

Nelson Mandela the hero of the century,
The one who brought democracy to South Africa,
He planted a seed,
Now a tree has grown,
And that is why there is a new South Africa.

Surita Chaboolall

Nelson Mandela is one super guy

He's sometimes so friendly
And sometimes so shy.
He's loved and respected, wherever he goes
For his kind, gentle nature
And the wisdom that grows.
He's met all kinds of people,
North, South, East and West
But always returns to the land he loves best.
He supports all our sportsmen at all the big games
Shakes all their hands and remembers their names.
He hugs little children like a real old grandpa
And they hug him back like a big sweetie jar.
All countries want to have a great leader
But none come close to our own MADIBA.

Emma Fairclough
(Age 11)

Artwork by Chanadia Stigling, 11 years

31

Artwork by Nomvula Masina

Boy you must have a lot of stamina!

Lenasia

29 October 2001

Dearest Madiba

I hope with the grace of God that you are in the best of health. I sometimes wonder how at your age you carry out your workload. Boy you must have a lot of stamina! Please share your secret with me.

I am a proud citizen of this land South Africa, a place of joy and sorrow, happiness, sadness and beauty. All around us is beauty, the lovely flower of no value may be small but in many ways it is big in its beauty. All around us every day new life is formed, but at the same time the yellow ferocious lion catches the newly born kudu who was having a first and last peep at the world.

Driving through town we see massive skyscrapers, people scuttling here and there thinking "hurry, hurry, faster". As you drive on into the cool night there are fewer and fewer of these huge ugly masses of concrete. Bird choirs sing of prettiness and happiness. Owls hoot while out hunting. The smell of pollution and the noise has all evaporated. It feels as though you are in a dream.

South Africa is rich but at the same time poor. If you think about it we are rich in the area of agricultural things, but we are poor in happiness. All around us people's faces are made up of scowls and our mouths utter harsh words. Everyday the newspapers are filled with ugliness and frightful things. It's all bomb blasts, war, arguments, death and sadness. South Africa is a beautiful place, but it is also sad and always will be if we don't help – together.

Thank you for taking the time and effort to read my letter. May God bless you and spare you so you will have a long and healthy life for all the children of South Africa to benefit from.

With lots of hugs and kisses

Zahraa Patel

Artwork by Tiffany Smith, Grade 1

33

work by Sithembiso Mqadi, 13 years

My dream is to meet you and Mrs Graça in person

Artwork by Larissa Moodley, 8 years

Germiston

27 August 2001

Dear Madiba

One of my greatest dreams is to become a singer with my group called Velvet Ice. We always thought of becoming international singers. We write our own songs and we spend a great deal of time studying and writing songs.

My other dream is to meet you and Mrs Graça in person. It is a great honour to be writing this letter. You started off as a young dreamer. You made your dreams come true and you fought for freedom, peace and humanity and love. You said we're a rainbow nation and we are.

You are a man of power and peace and love. I will honour you and give you a great deal of respect for what you did for our country. Keep up the excellent work you are still doing.

Love

Dineo Masipa

(Grade 7)

Artwork by Mabhungu Sindile, Grade 2

35

Having cancer does not mean it's the end of your life

Dear Mr Mandela

I am writing this letter to you to tell you how proud I am to be a South African. First of all thank you very much for sacrificing your life for us. I really think everybody loves you for that. I've wished to meet you since I was a little girl. Especially because of my two brothers: my one brother, Ibrahim, was born when you came out of prison on 11 February 1990 and my other brother, Abubacar, was born when you became president on 10 May 1994.

I'm very sorry you have cancer but I still love you very much. Having cancer does not mean it's the end of your life. I really hope you get to read my letter.

With love

Aisha Margolis

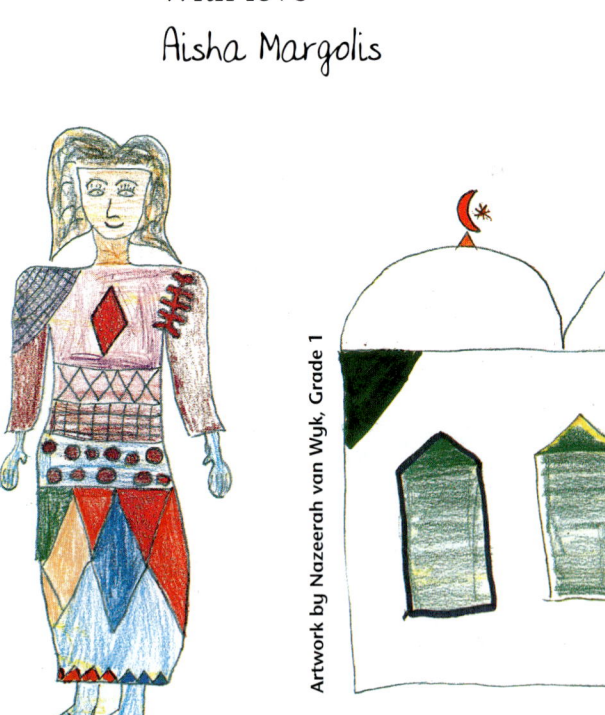

Artwork by Nazeerah van Wyk, Grade 1

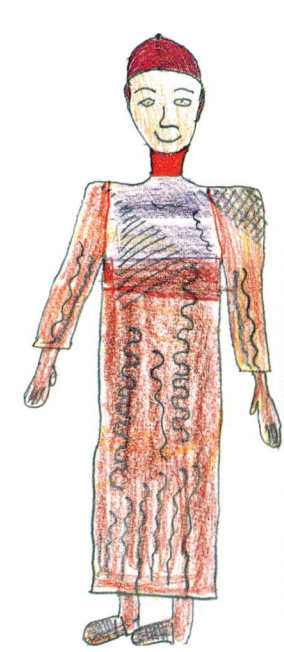

Artwork by Angelique Ferreira, 8 years

Dear Madiba

I am fortunate I never experienced apartheid. Because of you I know I never will. You gave away 27 years of your life so unselfishly, so that the country of your birth and my birth is free for all its people to enjoy.

I only heard about apartheid from my parents and from the stories that I've read. I know I don't understand it but I'm sure it must have been bad.

Our country has been blessed by its natural beauty, the mountains, streams, wild life and beaches that have been kissed by the African sun.

Because of your sacrifice, our country is now open for all to enjoy, and not like before when only a few could enjoy it. I love our own rainbow nation. Thank you, Madiba. Nkosi sikelelel' iAfrika.

Tasneem Moosajee

(Grade 4)

Dear Madiba

In 27 year's time I will be 38 years old. I cannot imagine this, it seems such a long time away. I hope to be head boy next year, and follow the same course as my elder brother. I would then go to university and study medicine. I will work hard at my studies because I want to be an outstanding doctor. I will find time for parties, girls and I hope to be comfortably well off and to drive my dream car a BMW Z3. All this in 27 year's time!

I stop, I wait, I think! Did you have this dream? You gave us 27 years of your life. Your dreams were shattered. Your personal life and goals put on hold. You gave your life so that I may have mine. I grow up in a South Africa that is taking baby steps towards peace. I believe that my generation will fulfil your dream. You have given me a chance to go where I want to and to be what I want to be.

By your sacrifice South Africa is now a world player. There is no other place I'd rather be than here. The violence and crime is a blight on your vision for this country, but, Madiba, I am going to make every effort to fight for peace. You have brought about awareness in my country of its cultures and its people. This has made me a better person.

Madiba, you have shown the world the importance and the power of a child. You have pledged your support to the children of South Africa. You are our role model. If all children model themselves on you South Africa will be a leader of nations.

Your famous smile and jive is recognised the world over. Wherever you go you make people smile, forget their problems and become friendlier. Thank you, Madiba, for giving us a great start in life. I wish you happiness and strength in your golden years.

Love

Kyle J Pillay
(Age 11)

Artwork by Nomvelo Zungu, 8 years

What it means to be a South African!

Being a South African
doesn't mean that you
have to drive a
fancy car or live in
a big house.

Being a South African
means to be united
and to love one another
to live in unity as brothers.

Nelson Mandela

Thank you Nelson
Mandela. We'll remember
Nelson Mandela he
brought back hope
to South Africa there
are no more wars now.

When the people knew
that Nelson Mandela
was out of jail they
had a song:
Oh! Nelson Mandela
he brought back
hope to South Africa.
I am proud to be
a South African.

Marie Bopape
(Grade 6)

Artwork by Smita Waghmarae, Grade 6

I AM PROUD TO BE A SOUTH AFRICAN CHILD

Artwork by Zinhle Ngidi, Grade 7

Grandfather to us all

I'm proud to be South African
Our rainbow's clear and bright
Look at the end and you will see
Our cultures can unite.
Madiba, Nelson
A friend to us all
A face of the nation
You heard our call
Freedom for everyone
Votes for us all
A friend of the children
Grandfather to us all.
I'm proud to be South African
Together we can stand
Let's fight the crime, the hijacking
And save our beautiful land.

Stephanie Jooste
(Grade 4)

Artwork by Zandre Swart, 8 years

Weltevreden Park
Florida

Dear Nelson Mandela

I'm a child of this glorious rainbow nation. I love the artists' beadwork, the dancing, the South African night sky, the story of old Africa (for example Ndebele, San, first gold, etc.), the sunny skies and the excellent game reserves, with the lions, leopards, buck, cheetah, birds, giraffe, wild dogs, hyena and much much MUCH more. I also like the sport except when Hansie gave us a bad name. The rugby's good but so is the golf. I think we should participate in more sport. Well that's my opinion.

From your fan

Chelsea

Ocean View

25 October 2001

Dear Madiba

My name is Tamzyn Thomas. I am 12 years old and in Grade 6. I admit I am not your average 12-year-old girl. First of all, I love my school and doing orals in front of my class (in English and in Afrikaans). I am not grossed out that quickly or frightened of other people. I hate makeup because it covers the beautiful faces that God has given us.

I am writing to tell you how proud I am to live in this wonderful land that you have made a nation. I have always been proud of having such a gracious role model as yourself.

I was in the crowd when you spoke in Cape Town in 1994. I don't remember much, but people started shooting at the crowd.

Madiba, you are a role model to the world and I am proud to be of the same country as the man who practically awakened the world.

I also love writing letters, stories and poems.

That's all from my pen and I.

Peace and love

Tamzyn Thomas
(Grade 6)

Artist unknown

I can go to any school and use any library

Extension One
Protea Glen

4 September 2001

Dear Mr Nelson Mandela

South Africa is blessed to have had a leader like you. Sir, you have helped to bring about change and that is why today I'm proud to be South African.

The changes you have helped to bring about in our country are remarkable because today, as a black person, I can go to any school and use any library and that makes me really proud to live in this country.

With your determination, sir, you paid the price by spending your youth in a dark cell on Robben Island but today I can study and prepare for a bright future. As a result of what you did racism and discrimination and insults are breaking down and I am very proud of that! In the early sixties and seventies our country was dark with blood of heroes like Hector Petersen, but now it is bright and colourful again. We have different cultures, languages and attitudes in one nation.

Mr Mandela, you have been a hero to millions and as you are South African, I'm more than proud to be South African too.

Yours sincerely

Suzette Masondo

Artwork by Amy, Grade 5

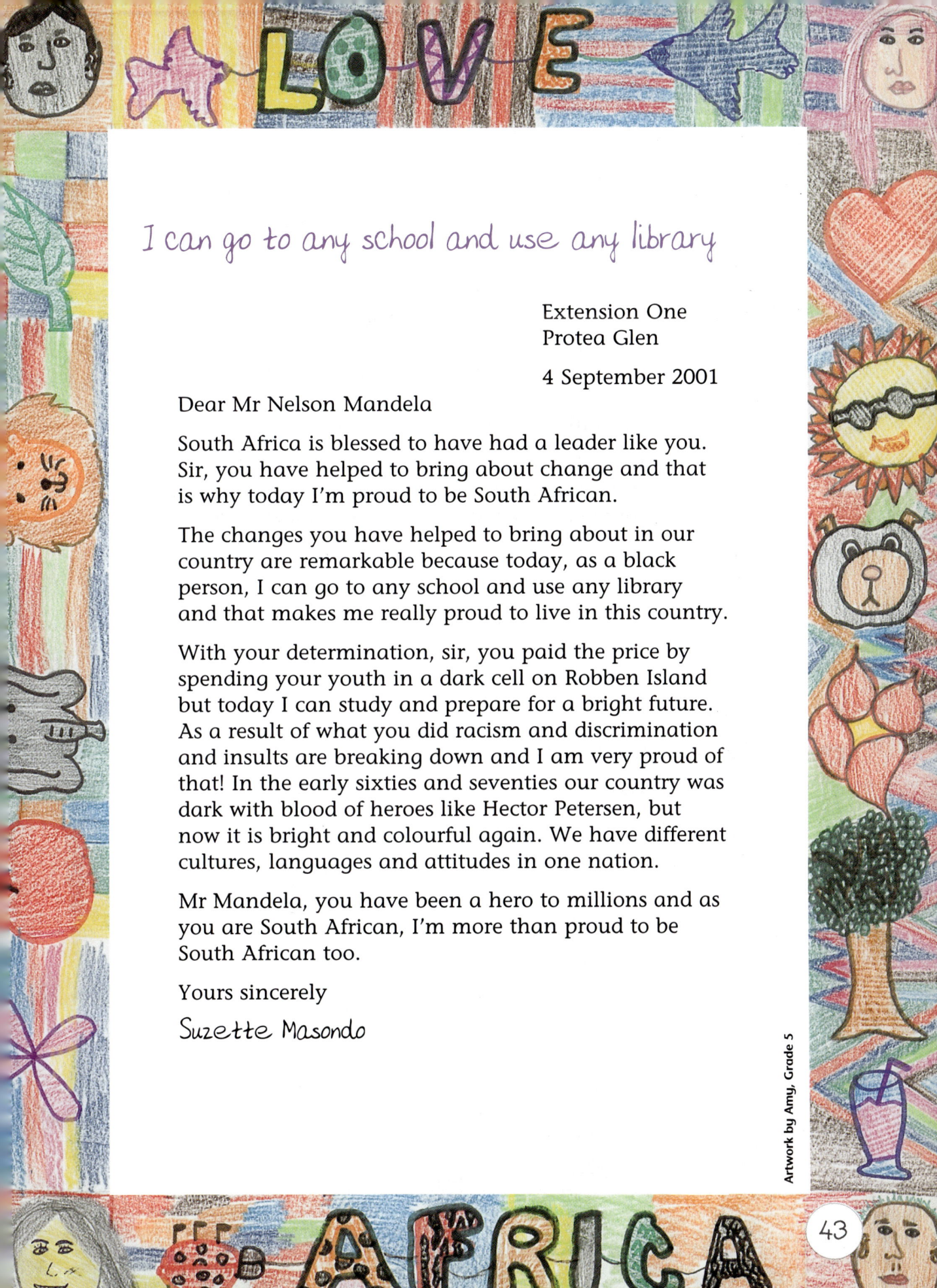

port Elizabeth
2001-10-19

Dear Madiba

I am proud of my colour.

I am proud two be in South African.

I am very proud two be here.

I am very happy two be in this country

from Kurt

Letter and artwork by Kurt Bagoes, 7 years

There were no bridges but now we can cross nicely.

Dear Grandpa Madiba

You are so great. I am proud of you. Many children of my age are being cared for because of you. You changed this country so it can be loved. My parents dreamed that I would be able to go to a good school and now I can. So you are a person to be praised. One day I would like just to touch and hug you, that's my dream. You care for those who are helpless. You feed those who are hungry. I love you Nelson Mandela. I love the way you work and your attitude, the way you love children and they love you too. I just love you to bits just as Mrs Naidoo says to the lovely children in the class. One day I would like to be just like you. The time you spent in jail was a way for us to get freedom. When you came out everybody in South Africa was free. Everyone likes to be a South African. You are building schools for children. Children had to walk long distances to school but now schools are nearer for them.

You also brought clinics for sick people and those who could not walk long distances. Those places where they were had no roads. Now they are free to walk from place to place. There were no bridges but now we can cross nicely.

Madiba, while you were in jail this country was shaking. People were killing each other.

May God give you more and more long life. Thank you, Grandpa. I am proud of my country.

I love you.

Noxolo Qwabe

(Grade 3)

Artwork by Chelsea, Grade 5

I am proud to be a minor citizen

Dear Madiba

My name is Nasreen Adams. I am in Gauteng and proud to be a minor citizen of our country. Excluding all the negative things of course. First of all the climate here is great. There are long hot days and cool showers of rain to end the days. No wonder the Europeans and English come to South Africa for the lovely weather, our nature and our wildlife. Tourism brings a lot of money to the country. We should support organisations that protect our wildlife especially our endangered animals.

I am a Coloured Muslim. My culture is Islam. South Africa is rich in different cultures and languages. I guess that is why we have 11 official languages.

I am very proud that South Africa hosted the world conference against racism. Maybe it was because of how some brave South Africans fought against racism. Some of those brave people were Mahatma Ghandi, and you our very own Madiba, and many more. So South Africa has a very rich history too.

The HIV/Aids epidemic is a very serious concern in our country. I hope that I can make a difference by educating more people about what I know about the virus. I think that when more people know how serious this virus can be that it can start decreasing.

So you see why I am proud to be a South African child living in this great country. As the saying goes, we have braaivleis, rugby, sunny skies and Chevrolet.

Yours truthfully

Nasreen Adams

my condolences for the loss of a good friend of yours, Govan Mbeki

11 September 2001

Dear Mr Mandela

Greetings and how are you under the beautiful African sun? Anyway, I thought I should introduce myself. I am Nwabisa Maqungo and I am from Samuel Nongogo Primary School in Port Elizabeth.

I just wanted to tell you that you are my idol and I would really love to meet you someday. I would like to send my condolences for the loss of a good friend of yours, Govan Mbeki.

Maybe next time you come to Port Elizabeth you can come visit our school. We would really appreciate it because the school needs all the sponsors it can get.

I hope you find a cure for cancer because it would be a great loss to the whole country if there were no cure for you. The other day I was thinking about how it is to be like you. You are probably the most important person in South Africa and I like the way you marketed the county when you were president.

If I were the president for one day I would make that day a public holiday in honour of what you have done for us.

Yours sincerely

Nwabie girl

(Grade 6)

Artwork by Catherine Attridge

47

Artwork by Paul Kwele, Grade 6

Artwork by Lebogo Mokatse, Grade 6

Artwork by Angel Zulu, Grade 6

Artwork by Mishlin Pillay, 8 years

Artwork by Thandoka Zimnyungu

Artwork by Karen Govender, 10 years

Artwork by Tyron Fowler, Grade 4

Artwork by Nondumiso Nldlela, 12 years

49

Artwork by Thato Nkosi, 7 years

Montford
Chatsworth

Dear Mr Nelson Mandela

I am so very pleased to write to you. I am also proud to be called a South African child and there are many reasons why.

I was born and brought up in KwaZulu/Natal South Africa. South Africa has so many wonderful tourist sights. If I were a tourist I would tell everyone I knew to come live in South Africa.

Mr Nelson Mandela, I think that you are a wonderful man. I would like to tell you that I think the Nelson Mandela Children's Fund is the greatest idea that any person could think of. You thought of all the children in South Africa that are without shelter and food. Your children's fund is really working miracles for some children and families.

Some people and children, including myself, think you are a living legend. I hope you come to Chatsworth to visit us again. Thank you for having the letter-writing competition. It gives me a great opportunity to write to you. I would like to meet you in person and get to know you well.

Thank you for taking the time to think of us children. I will always look up to you as my role model and as my hero.

Yours faithfully

Michelle Naicker

(Your number 1 fan)
(Grade 5)

Artwork by Stephen-John Martin

I am certain you do not remember me

Robertsham

Dear Mr Mandela

I am certain you do not remember me, but you held me in your arms when I was three months old. Mum still talks about what a proud moment it was. I am a great admirer of yours.

You have achieved so much in your life and have done so much for our beautiful country. A person like you deserves every happiness in the world. When I heard of your recent illness it tore at my heart. I hope you get better soon, for like me, the rest of the world is praying for you.

Best wishes

Faheem Khota

(Grade 6)

Artwork by Wendy Manxayile, 10 years

Greyville

18 October 2001

Dear Mr Mandela

Being a South African has made me realise that there is more to life than just dreaming about something. Instead of wishing, I should go out and do something good for myself and others no matter how small it is, at least I'll know that I've followed a dream and I've made an achievement that I am proud of. I am prepared to make something of myself.

There is pride and joy in South Africa.

Yours sincerely

Nomzamo Nxumalo

(Grade 5)

Port Elizabeth

Dear Mr Madiba

How are you today? I am fine. I want to know what it is like to be a president. I want to be a president like you. I hope you read this letter Mr Madiba. I write this letter to show I care about you.

I wish you could visit my school. I wish you could see my mother. She found a new job and I am proud of her. My father does not work. I wish he could find a new job too. How did you become a president Mr Mandela?

From

Lungile Dladla

(Grade 6)

Artwork by Camille Davies, Grade 3

Artwork by Ziyaad Raban, Grade 5

A Child of Africa

People say 'Africa, a continent plagued by poverty, war
and disease'

But don't be deceived about what lies south of the
Mediterranean Sea.

Because in this vastly beautiful land,
Lies more than animals, plants and sand.

In Africa I see
A land, that sets me free.

In this land I always find
A history strong powerful and yet kind.

Which foretells an Africa of strength and power,
That sparkles with happiness and peaceful showers.

Because Africa is so tame and yet so wild,
I will always be a proud African Child.

Deena Dinat
(Grade 6)

Artwork by Somkelo Naki

Artwork by Nomvula Mtshali, Grade 7

55

We can overcome the most difficult hurdles in life

Crawford

24 October 2001

Dear Mr Mandela

I am proud to be a South African child because I was born in South Africa. South Africa has great tourist attractions, mineral wealth (gold, diamonds) and agriculture. It therefore holds a great future for all South African children. Our country is so beautiful that it brings in tourists. Tourism brings work for people. Now that apartheid is gone we have better education for all and opportunities that we did not have before. That is another reason why I am proud to be a South African child today.

People in South Africa are very friendly. They come from many cultural and religious backgrounds and are very tolerant of these differences.

You are my role model because you brought us through very difficult times into the light. And you did it, most importantly, in a peaceful manner. By being kind, caring, passive and non-violent you have shown us that we can overcome the most difficult hurdles in life. You are also a very giving man. If for this reason only, I am proud to be a South African child.

Kindest regards

Rizia Essack

(Grade 6)

Artwork by Kelly Lisa Kirstnasamy, Grade 2

First comes God, my mom, my dad, then you, Lance Klusner and Brian Baloyi

Greyville

18 October 2001

Dear Mr Mandela

I admire you a lot because you fought for us and won at the end. I feel sorry for the people who put you in jail. You are my role model. First comes God, my mom, my dad, then you, Lance Klusner and Brian Baloyi.

There is no war in South Africa. That is why I am proud to be a citizen of South Africa. In Mozambique there was a flood and we helped them, in India there was an earthquake and we helped them too. There are nice people in South Africa and you are the best president I ever knew and I thank you for your hard work.

Yours sincerely

Thabiso Mbatha

(Grade 5)

Artwork by Grant Henderson, Grade 7

Dear Mr Mandela

I'm proud of our flag. It has the best pattern and the best colours in the whole world. The weather is always sunny. Thank you for looking after all the children. You are a kind man. From Chloe

Letter and artwork by Chloe, Grade 2

25 October 2001

Dear Madiba

I love my country. I love you. I like to be a South African because I'm meant for it. I wish that in our country there would be peace. And no guns and knives so we cannot kill each other because there are just too many people that we are losing. From Aids and cancer.

We hope that everyone in this world can greet each other with a smile so that they cannot be fighting because fighting is destroying our world. I'm sending this letter not just for you it is for everybody in the world so we can stop fighting and killing each other and swearing to another person.

Sinenhlanhla Mthethwa

(Grade 3)

Artwork by John Shamshum, 7 years

Artwork by Justine O'Neale, 9 years

Artwork by Nankululeko Mbatha, 12 years

Artwork by Sheree O'Donoghue, 9 years

Artwork by Obriek Lukali

Artwork by Larissa Moodley, 8 years

Artwork by Duane Hanwith-Horden, 9 years

Artwork by Martin Mamabolo, Grade 6

Artwork by Jacobus Breytenbach, Grade 7

Kwa-Dwesi
Port Elizabeth

Dear Mr Mandela

I am fine thanks wishing you the same.

My name is Sithembele Mavata. I am nine years old.

I stay in Port Elizabeth with my parents and two brothers. My first brother is in Grade 9 and he wants to be a doctor. He can because he is the master of maths. My second brother is in Grade 6. He also wants to be a doctor. I for one I want to be a president.

The reason I write this letter is because I want to know how to make an application for being a president. Please write down and show me how I must write my Curriculum Vitae if I want to be a president. I also want to know what subjects I must do and how many degrees I must have.

Please Mr Mandela can you answer my letter as soon as possible.

Yours faithfully

Sithembele Mavata

(Age 9)

22 October 2001

Dear Madiba

I am happy to go to school and learn and also play with my friends at school. But when I watch the news on TV, I feel so sad when I see people dying and the wars that happen in places and sometimes I also start to cry a lot. Madiba, please can you help and tell them to stop the wars?

Penny Naidoo

(Grade 3)

Artwork by Simone Matthews

Artwork by Sadija Manuel

Chatsworth

Dear Mr Madiba

My name is Kenton. I am 12 years old. I attend a special school for the disabled.

My only dream for my school is to get a new bus sponsor for our school. I cannot attend school regular as our bus breaks down all the time. This is causing me to loose out on my special education. I wish my dream can come true.

Kenton Govender

Artwork by Aviwe Mwali, 7 years

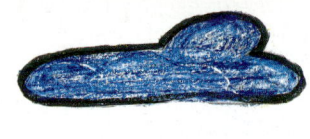   

Artwork by Irfaan Bey, 12 years

Lenasia South

Dear Madiba

The weather in Johannesburg has been quite warm with plenty of rain.

I am very concerned about South Africa's future. Last week Thursday around the corner from my house a woman was shot dead on the spot and nothing was done about it. South Africa is getting worse by the day. The rand has no value. Madiba, when you were released 11 years ago we thought that we would have a better South Africa. More people are dying and more crime has been going on and I would appreciate it if you could see to the matter as I am still proud to be a South African with you around.

From

Aslam Shafi

(Grade 3)

 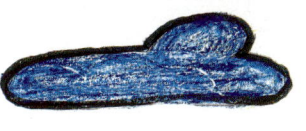  

Durban

12 November 2001

Dear Madiba

I love South Africa because there are a lot of sights to see, places to be and people to meet. I am proud of this country but there is a lot of crime against children like me, like kidnapping, raping and especially child abuse.

Tourists should enjoy and learn from our country's children. We are a rainbow nation and children belong to the nation as well. Being a child in South Africa is better than being a child at sea. I am glad I live in South Africa because I also have rights just like the older people in South Africa.

If I had three wishes about the children of South Africa I would wish that ...

1) every child would have a home and a family

2) every child would be safe from crime and

3) children would be accepted for who they really are, instead of what they look like.

Oh yes! Before I forget, you are my hero and my role model.

God bless you Madiba and may he be with you forever.

Yours faithfully

Melissa Rachael Morgan

(Grade 5)

Artwork by Sithalima

all South African boys and girls are Madiba's children

Umlazi Township
Ntokozweni

Dear Dr Madiba

I am a South African. I was born a decade ago in South Africa. This is my home.

I remember five years ago when I went to my grandfather's plaas. I was there for one week but it felt like only one day. We took the long way there since there was no short way. One day my grandfather and I took cattle to graze the greener pastures. The next morning I had an opportunity to milk the cows. I even drank the cow's milk straight from the mammary glands. How warm the milk was! On the last day when the sun was setting in the afternoon, my grandfather and I rode on horses and my grandfather was herding the cattle. I'll never forget those happy moments with my late grandfather – he was the calmest person I've ever known.

In 1999 I went to Switzerland, Malta and Holland during the school holidays. At the Maltese Museum we had to produce our passports. On leaving the museum the security guard said, "Pass my regards to Mr Mandela". How stunned I was to realise how well known our Madiba is!

As if that was not enough, after that I went to Zurich. My mum took me to a Swiss school and three girls came to me and said, "Are you Mr Mandela's granddaughter?" I said, "Yes." And then a little moment later I thought to myself that all South African boys and girls are Madiba's children anyway.

On my return to South Africa I was happy when the aeroplane landed at Johannesburg airport, I saw a large poster reflecting Mandela smiling. Oh! How proud I felt, at being able to identify with an internationally acclaimed hero like Dr Madiba.

Yes, I was back in South Africa (I was back home) – a home I share with Dr Mandela.

Thembeka Mtuli

(Grade 5)

Artwork by Sinoxolo Hoko, 12 years

Crosby

10 September 2001

Dear Madiba

I am Peter Ramatuele, a boy from a South Sotho tribe. Presently I live in Crosby in the Gauteng Province but I was born in the North West Province.

South Africa is a country that has a rich history. You were one of the people that made it so rich and colourful. By forgiving your enemies you gave a good example to the rest of the world when you came out of jail. You became a well-respected president.

The only problems facing this country are the crime rate and Aids. Some of the things that lead to these problems are:

• The youth don't have self-esteem. They are too busy trying to impress their friends.

• The youth turn to drugs when they have problems.

• Drugs lead to carelessness and young people have unprotected sex with their partners, or they even turn to crime.

These are just some of the reasons we have problems. Thank you.

Yours sincerely

Peter Ramatuele

Artwork by Sirshay Rampersadh, 10 years

Durban

Dear Nelson Mandela

Hello Nelson Mandela. My name is Siphesihle and my surname is Ngcobo. You are the only president that I love Nelson Mandela. I also love you because our birthdays only have one different day. Your birthday is on 18 July and my birthday is on 19 July. So we are friends.

When you came out of prison no one can beat you in being a president. You made people use one toilet, beach, bathroom and school.

Siphesihle Ngcobo
(Grade 3)

November 2001

Dear Mr Mandela

South Africa is a very beautiful place to live in. Madiba, you gave us the right to be free of apartheid and the right to vote. You also gave us the freedom to speak.

I would like to ask you if you could help the poor people. Many children in our country are suffering from abuse by their parents and their grandparents. I wish you could do something about it. Also the disabled and the people that have no work at all need help. If they have no work then there is a lot of crime in our country. Please Mr Mandela if you could help us I would really appreciate it.

Thank you very much.

Siddeeqa Petersen
(Grade 4)

Artwork by Phumlani

Dear Madiba

My name is Nosisa Banda. I am 10 years old. Sometimes I see
you on television having fun with children and in meetings.
I love you Madiba because you are like a father to children.
I just wish I would be right there with you. You are a miracle.
Sometimes when it is my birthday I long for
you to be there but I don't know how.

Nosisa Banda

(Grade 3)

Our new South Africa, with all its joy,
Brings happiness to every girl and boy.
A rainbow nation, under one "umbrella"
Brought about by my man, Mr Mandela.
The national anthem song
Is kept dear to our hearts for so long
It's no wonder, why, a guy like me
Would be so proud undoubtedly,
To live in perfect harmony,
In South Africa, what a country!!!

Nivesh Sing
(Grade 4)

Artwork by Sibonga Ncanana, 12 years (border), Tracey Chuma (springbok), artist of flag unknown

Merebank
Durban

To the father of South Africa, Mr Nelson Mandela

In the past, I have always been proud of my culture, but a little ashamed of my country. The leaders of the old South Africa never really set examples for children to follow. They led the children to hate each other due to the colour of skin.

The entire world condemned our country for the injustices that were taking place. Our people were crying for a person who would free them. This person came in the form of a man known worldwide as Madiba. We the children of South Africa have a new outlook on life now and faith that we can overcome anything!

Thank you Mr Mandela for being a father and a role model.

Yours sincerely

Suraya M
(Grade 7)

Artwork by Karissa Moodley, 12 years

Artwork by Choki Lubabalo Nxele Mabi

Artwork (Africa) by Kuhle, 10 years

Dear Nelson Mandela and friends

I am very glad to be a child of Africa.

For when I am sad, Africa you help me.
When I am lonely, Africa you comfort me.
When I am mean, Africa you stop me.
Africa, you are the best thing
that has happened to me and my family!
So I want to thank you for the birds
and the bees and our air from trees,
and most of all for me,
that I am a child of Africa.

Amy
(Grade 5)

Artwork (Earth and flag) by Sipho Zwane

Pinetown

22 November 2001

Dear Mr Mandela

I am writing to tell you how proud I am to live in South Africa. I am proud of our sportsmen and sportswomen. Our soccer players go overseas to play against other countries and even if they are beaten I will always be proud of my South African team. I am proud of the people that make wheat so there can be something like bread to eat everyday. I am proud of the cows that make milk that we put on our cereal. And for the people that make money so our parents can pay for our school fees.

I am proud of our country because they give us advice about HIV and Aids. I am proud of the people that have courage to work in mines so we can get gold, diamonds and the other things. I am proud because I get clean water and electricity. I am proud of the police that stop the violence and crime in our country. And I like to thank you for stopping the apartheid between the blacks and whites.

Yours faithfully

Khethu Ngcobo

(Grade 7)

Artwork by Tsoni Melikhaya, Grade 6

A proud African child!!

Africa, a wonderful and beautiful continent! I know that because I am an African child, and that's who I am. I am proud and happy every day when I think of our continent, our history, and our people who fought for liberty and freedom of expression – as well as for every individual to be treated with respect and dignity.

From a continent that was once a free-for-all jungle now civilised, comes this proud African child. I am proud about my culture, language, roots and who I am. Africa is no typical place: it has fascinating wildlife, attractive plant species and a unique environment. Interesting animals live here. Africa is the home of the big five!

A proud African child, that is who I am. Africa is Africa because of US.

Palesa Ratsomo

Artwork by Jacqueline

74

Artwork by Nati Trassierra, Grade 5

Lenasia

30 October 2001

Dear Madiba

Hello Madiba! It's almost 11 years since your release. I was barely a year old. I was born into a new South Africa with you as its leader. As the years went by my parents enlightened me about what life was like in the old South Africa. As I grew up and entered school life I realised how thankful I should be.

For the first time we had racially mixed schools. We learned about different cultures and began understanding each other. The international community accepted us with open arms. We tasted, lived and appreciated the freedom that you fought for. We are living and enjoying our freedom with you, the greatest freedom fighter of the century. And that makes me proud to be a South African.

Forever your loyal supporter

Ameera Seedat

(Age 12)

Dear Mr Mandela

You proved that no matter how bad your past may have been your future can still be bright. You gave people inspiration and motivation to strive to achieve the best in their lives.

Lee-Ann Balana

(Grade 7)

Dear Mr Mandela

I want say: Don't do crime. Crime is bad. And stop the war and have peace in South Africa and wherever I go my heart will say I'm a South African child.

Cebo Ndlovu

(Grade 5)

Dear Mr Nelson Mandela

We have a vast number of cultures and languages in South Africa and some are very complicated but interesting to learn. South Africans are very friendly people but some choose crime as their option to get out of whatever life they have.

If I go to another country, I will be proud to say: "I am South African" and I am proud of my father for raising me and I am proud to have a loving family to support me.

Phumelele Sindisiwe Sibisi

Dear Mr Mandela

You are an inspiration to many citizens. You made many races become one nation. You made many of our dreams come true. As a "black" citizen I now can venture into the "white" only places. With many thanks to you I can now proudly say I am a South African!

Bongile Myeza

(Grade 7)

Dear Mr Mandela

We have a wonderful community in South Africa. We have fantastic weather. Sometimes the weather is unpredictable. Now there's only two problems with South Africa: the crime and the pollution. But you get that in other countries as well.

Love

Puleng Stewart

Dear Madiba

When you came out of jail, you shook the hands of the people who put you there that's why you are my hero!

Yours sincerely

Taariq Jaffer

(Age 12)

Dear Mr Madiba

South Africa has beautiful flowers and animals and nice people who make it even better. It has the most interesting background. It is a forgiving country with tolerance and reconciliation. There is no apartheid anymore and everyone is fair and square. Our country has become wonderful because of an old, nice, friendly and helping man called Mr Madiba.

Xoliswa Skosana

(Age 9)

Dear Madiba

Some people say South Africa is poor but it has a rich heart. South Africa is a proud country. That is why I like being a South African.

Lungelo Nomvete

Artwork by Puleng Stewart

port Elizabeth
2001-10-19

Dear Madiba
I am Proud of My colour
I am proud to be a
south African child

thank you   from Live to you

I am Live
Mda

Letter and artwork by Live Mde, 7 years

I see you on TV but I do not see you in real life

Dear Madiba

My name is Zandalee. I am 7 years old. I am in Grade 1.
I hope you are better now. Every time I see you on TV but
I do not see you in real life.

I am proud to be a South African. You were the first black
president in South Africa. You spent 27 years in prison.
When you came out of prison you made so much changes
in our country. And you have built the Mandela's Children
Fund. You are so loving and caring to every single person.

Yours sincerely

Zandalee

(Grade 1)

Artwork by Nabeel Badat, 8 years

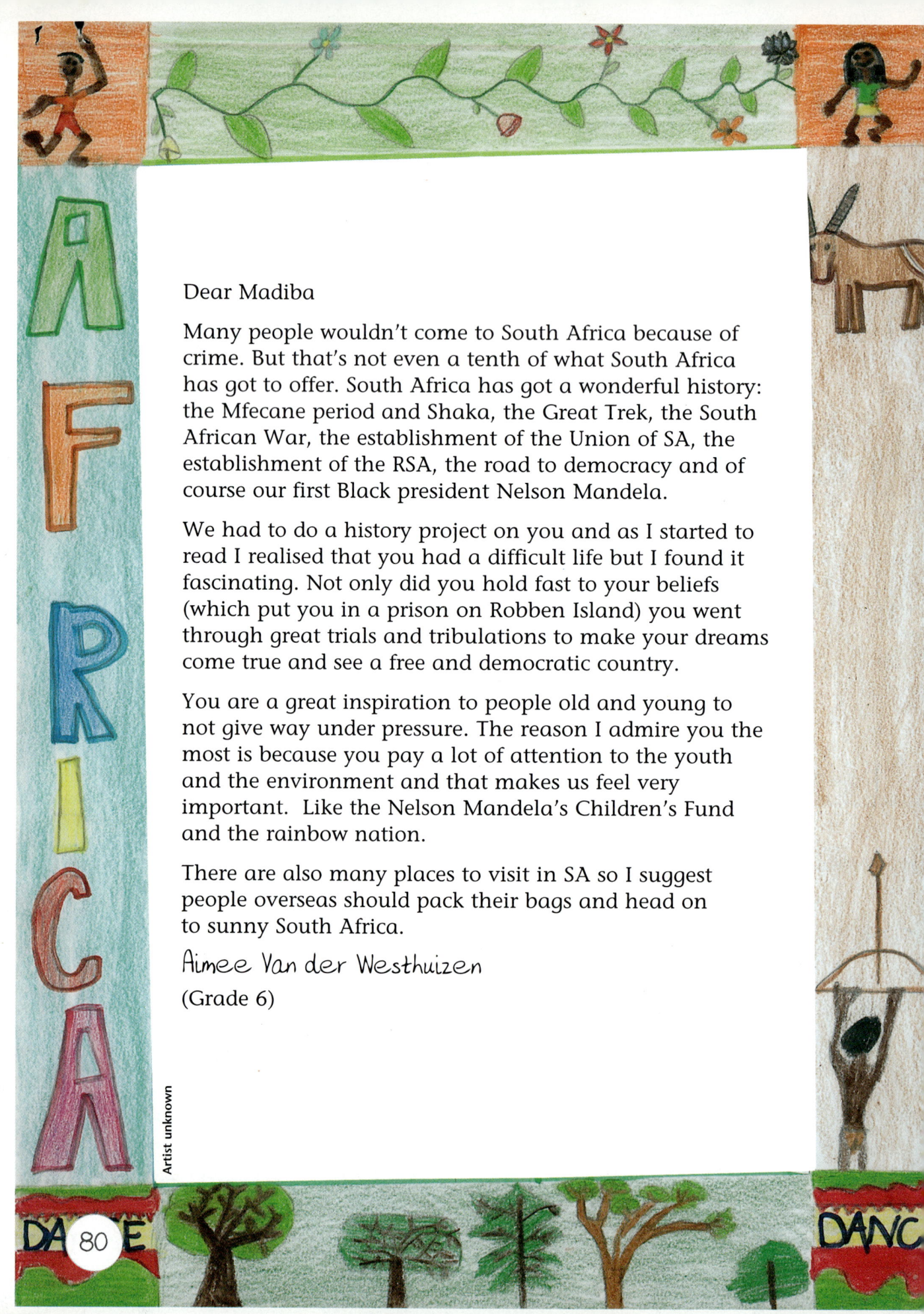

Dear Madiba

Many people wouldn't come to South Africa because of crime. But that's not even a tenth of what South Africa has got to offer. South Africa has got a wonderful history: the Mfecane period and Shaka, the Great Trek, the South African War, the establishment of the Union of SA, the establishment of the RSA, the road to democracy and of course our first Black president Nelson Mandela.

We had to do a history project on you and as I started to read I realised that you had a difficult life but I found it fascinating. Not only did you hold fast to your beliefs (which put you in a prison on Robben Island) you went through great trials and tribulations to make your dreams come true and see a free and democratic country.

You are a great inspiration to people old and young to not give way under pressure. The reason I admire you the most is because you pay a lot of attention to the youth and the environment and that makes us feel very important. Like the Nelson Mandela's Children's Fund and the rainbow nation.

There are also many places to visit in SA so I suggest people overseas should pack their bags and head on to sunny South Africa.

Aimee Van der Westhuizen

(Grade 6)

Artist unknown

Artwork by Linda Tsele, Grade 7

Artwork by Sabathile Shandu, Grade 5

Aids

A very bad disease
It is killing South Africa.
And as a South African
child I want something
to be done
about it. Many
People are being
killed.
Please
Help.

Sabathile Shandu
(Grade 5)

Dear Madiba

I am writing to you because I would like to tell you how much I admired you as the president of our New South Africa. One thing that I admire most about you is the fact that although you were in prison for so long, it did not turn you into a bitter man.

Even though you are no longer our president, it makes me feel very proud to be South African when I watch CNN or other news channels and see the good work that you are doing to help other countries sort out their problems.

As a young teenage boy who loves the latest music and fashions, it's quite amazing to see how many famous singers, actors, actresses and politicians look up to you and respect you and value you as a person.

You are truly a remarkable man and I can only say that although you are no longer our president, in my eyes, and in many other South Africans' eyes, you are still our president!!

Yours sincerely

Ivan Jardim

(Age 13)

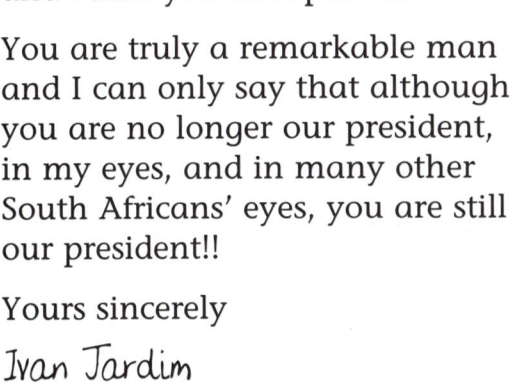

Artist unknown

83

Artwork by Derishka Ramlochan, Grade 3

I am colour-blind.

Dear Nelson Rolihlahla Mandela

I am proud that I was born in 1990, soon after you finally received your freedom. I am glad that when I was in my little cradle I could not just see my mom, but I could see her reach out and touch the hands of other children without seeing them as a different race, colour or creed. And finally, I am proud and glad that I was brought up to accept and live with everyone as my brother or sister. Not feeling hatred, jealousy and anger to people of other race groups brings much peace and joy to one's heart.

Everyone deserves the best in whatever they do. It is wonderful to know that when I finish school, I will not have to go far and wide to find a place to study or work. Every opportunity is open to everyone, thanks to you and the strong foundations you have laid. I am colour-blind. Even if God took away my eyesight it would not make a difference. Race, colour and creed are just words to describe the different people but LOVE conquers all and makes us equal. And in South Africa we have enough love to go around. All we have to do is share it.

I will not leave South Africa even if I could afford it one day. This is my home and I am here to stay. And because I am proud to live with everyone my heart bubbles with joy every morning when I wake up knowing that I am a South African!

Thank you

Anastasia Naidoo

(Age 11)

Artwork by Meghan Edward

I like school because it is better than sitting at home wasting your life on doing absolutely nothing.

Bethelsdorp
Port Elizabeth

24 October 2001

Dear Mr Mandela

My name is Jaylin Messeur, and I am eleven years old. I attend school at Bethvale Primary. My hobbies are swimming, singing and reading. I like school because it is better than sitting at home wasting your life on doing absolutely nothing. I also like sport because it keeps you fit and it can bring you far in life.

I am proud that we do not have any wars (and I hope we will never have any). And if we had wars I would not be proud of South Africa in any way. If I were an American or a Pakistani I would not be proud of the war that is taking place between them. I am also proud of you because you are always there for the people and children who need you.

What I really want is not only peace in our country but also peace in the world. I think that we can do it if we just love one another. I really like you Mr Mandela for all that you have done for South Africa. You are a very brave person.

Yours sincerely

Jaylin Messeur
(Age 11)

Artwork by Tarry Chambers, 7 years

4 September 2001

Dear Madiba

I am proud to be a South African child because in the past South Africa used to live in the apartheid system. Coloureds, Indians, black Africans were discriminated against. They were not allowed to go to parks, public toilets and malls. Black people had to carry dompasses every where they went. The education was terrible, but because there were people like you and Desmond Tutu, Mahatma Gandhi and many others (who never gave up hope for a better South Africa) education is better. I am now in Grade 7 and I attend a school in town where there are Indians, Whites, Coloureds and us black Africans.

I am also proud to be a South African child because of the women of this country. In the past women were discriminated against because of their sex (gender). A woman's place was always in the kitchen and in the mall to buy groceries. They were not even allowed to vote. But South African women put their feet down. They marched to the Union Buildings in Pretoria and made their voices heard. They wanted to do other things besides cleaning, cooking and looking after the babies. Thank you to the women of South Africa for your braveness. Women are growing. They own companies and are the breadwinners. People all over the world look up to South Africa and its brave citizens. South Africa might be small but it's full of great leaders and has a lot to offer.

Thank you Madiba and your helpers for giving us a better and brighter future.

Love always

Busisiwe Dlamini

(Grade 7)

Artwork by Michelle De Gouveia

87

Madiba
You have brought sunshine to my life

Letter and artwork by Mbali Hlongwa

Artwork by Allancia Naidoo, Grade 4

88

Katlehong

Dear Nelson Rolihlahla Mandela

I am very proud to be South African for many reasons. Thank you, Madiba, that we have freedom. Blacks and whites are united. I thank you for giving us the opportunity of education.

I love South Africa although it has a lot of crime, violence and abuse. South Africa is a better place now, thanks to you Madiba. I am proud of our cultures.

I know that you love children. Please help the needy people who love you because of what you did for South Africa, You were our inspiration. Did you know that you were my role model when you were president? You taught me lots of things like that we should love one another and care for each other. Madiba, you made so many people happy. You are still my role model. I realised that you are heaven-sent. You have been an inspiration to children in South Africa.

Madiba you've changed children's lives like mine. I would like to meet you someday and talk to you. Now that you're 83 may you see many many many more years.

God bless you

Ayanda Nkosi

(Grade 6)

Artwork by Nondiza Luganda, Grade 6

Eldorado Park
4 September 2001

Dear Mr Mandela

It is very important that you know how much South Africans are proud to be who they are. It is a special kind of pride because we overcame one of the biggest economical problems South Africa ever had, apartheid.

We are so very lucky that God blessed us with an angel like you, that's what I think you are: an angel sent by God to take away the pain and anger in our country. There are very few people on this earth that could do what you did. You forgave all those people who treated you like a dog. You could have got them back and reversed apartheid, but you didn't, you forgave them and rewarded them with love. You are a gift to this country and I believe your job is not done yet. I don't think any letter could explain in words the pride we have unless it is written from the heart. And I assure you that mine definitely is.

Wishing you years of joy and peace. You are as bright as a star.

A proud South African

Tunicia

Artwork by Clarissa Pillay, Grade 2

Letters, poems and art were created by children from these schools:

AL-AQSA School

Ashley Primary School

AYS Memorial Primary School

Bay Primary School

Berea West Preparatory School

Bethvale Primary School

Beverley Park Primary School

BJ Mnyanda Primary School

Bree Primary School

Clarence Primary School

Clayhaven Primary School

Cliffview Primary School

Cotswold Preparatory School

Daxina Primary School

Dinwiddie Primary School

Emafine Primary School

Emzomnoane Primary School

Gitanjali Primary School

Hartwell Private School

Hyde Park Primary

Innes Primary School

JN Tulwani Junior Primary School

Kommetjie Primary School

Morningside Primary School

Palmcroft Primary School

Panorama Primary School

Paul Sykes Primary School

Philip Nikiwe Primary School

Robertsham Primary School

Rosehill Junior Primary School

Sacred Heart College

Samuel Nongogo Primary School

Sea View Primary School

Settlers Primary School

Sophakama Primary School

Springfield Model Primary School

St Agnes RC Primary School

St Raphael's Special School

Summerwood Primary School

Susannah Fourie Primary School

Turfhall Primary School

Tyburn Primary School

Uitenhage Convent

Vredelust Primary School

Vuba Junior Primary School

Werda Junior Primary School

Willow Park Primary School

Thank you to the hundreds of other schools that took the time and care to enter the competition.

Artwork by Claudia, Grade 6

Ideas and activities for teachers and parents

By Cheryl Minkley

Dear Teachers and Parents

As you read this book, you will notice that it is far more than simply a collection of letters, poems and drawings. The book provides many learning opportunities and is a useful resource and source of inspiration for activities with children. Here are some ideas to get you started:

Reading *Letters to Madiba* with your children at home

Using *Letters to Madiba* with young children

- Ask very young children to tell you what they think some of the drawings mean and encourage them to make their own drawings.

- Select and read some of the letters and poems with your children. Let the children see the drawings and the text as you read. They can interpret the drawings.

- Many of the children write about Madiba as a grandfather. Your children could write and post letters to their grandparents or make cards for them. Ask the children to tell you what they can learn from their grandparents.

- Mr Nelson Mandela is also called Madiba. This is his clan name. Your children can find out what a clan name is and when it is used.

- Positive values are mentioned in some of the letters. This is a great opportunity to discuss values with your children. Do they agree with the letter-writers on pages 30 and 56 that kindness is important?

- Talk with your children about our animals, the climate, water, plants and many other topics that some of the children raised in their letters. You can read them stories and fables about animals and listen to stories they think up about animals.

- Ask your children to identify beautiful spots and also environmental problem areas in your region. Tell them what the area used to look like. They can give suggestions for improving the environment.

Using *Letters to Madiba* with older children

- Children can read the letters alone or with you. They can translate some of the letters to relatives who do not read English.

- There are many references to important events in the history of South Africa. Ask your children to find two or three references to historical events in the book. Discuss these with them.

Artwork by Tayron Barnard, Grade 1

- Read the letters on pages 6, 20, 46, 73 and 82 and find out what your children know about HIV/Aids. Talk about people you know who are living with HIV/Aids, and why it is important to respect them in the same way one respects all other people.

- Discuss the importance of facing the future with a positive attitude. Ask children to find letters in which Madiba's positive attitude is evident, and to decide how they can use his example in their own lives.

- Your children can tell you which letters and illustrations they like most. Ask them to choose one or two letter-writers with whom they think they would like to be friends. They can tell you why they chose them.

- Some of the letter-writers refer to problems in South Africa. Discuss some of these problems with your children. Ask them to find letters that show a positive approach to problems. What solutions can they suggest to problems like poverty, abuse and crime?

Reading *Letters to Madiba* at school

Using *Letters to Madiba* with learners in Grades 1 to 3

- Read a few of the letters and poems and plan fun activities and exciting, interesting discussions about them.

- Select and read two or three of the shorter, simpler letters (for example those on pages 76 and 77) to the learners. If possible, let learners see the text as you read, so that they become familiar with and begin to recognise certain words. Encourage them to draw their own illustrations for letters or poems.

- Certain letter-writers (like those on pages 40 and 45) refer to Madiba as a grandfather. In groups learners can tell each other about their grandparents and make cards for them. The school can organise a special day in honour of grandparents. Prepare activities for learners and their grandparents (for example, telling stories and showing each other crafts or skills) and help learners prepare entertainment (such as songs and short plays) for their grandparents.

Artwork (man) by Lucas Maseko

Artwork by Avisha

- The children who wrote the letters on pages 30 and 56 mention Mr Mandela's kindness. Discuss the importance of being kind to others and think of practical ways of doing this – at school and at home. What influence can being kind to others have on our country? Learners can list other values that they think are important.

- Ask learners to think about and write letters to a South African leader.

- Many letters mention environmental issues. Discuss some of these in class. Learners can find out more about some animals (where they live, sounds they make; what they look like, and so on); build clay models of animals; discuss wild animals and poisonous plants; find out about plants we use for food; plant seeds and grow vegetables; visit places where indigenous plants grow or where alien vegetation is being removed; make sundials or shadow sticks; or do experiments with water.

Using *Letters to Madiba* at school with learners in Grades 4 to 6

- Learners can read the letters alone, in pairs, or with you. If English is not their home language, read the letters with them and explain words and concepts they do not understand. Help them to work out the meanings of words from the context.

- Many of the children write about Mr Mandela as a role model. Discuss the reasons the writers of the letters on pages 42, 51, 56, 57, 70 and 89 give for Madiba being a role model. Learners can tell you who their role models are, and why, and you can tell them who inspires you, and why.

- Read the letter on pages 10 and 11 and ask learners to suggest what they would do, as president, to make South Africa a better place. They can take turns to be "president for a day" in class. The challenge for them is to make fair rules and practise democracy.

- Ask learners to tell you what they know about the history of our country and the struggle for democracy. Many letter-writers, born around the time of Mandela's release from prison, have no first-hand knowledge of apartheid. Learners can find out about some of the apartheid laws, people who were in prisons (including Mr Mandela) and life in "bantustans" or "locations". Discuss the meaning of democracy.

- Read the letters on pages 6, 20, 46, 73 and 82 and find out what your learners know about HIV/Aids. Visit a local clinic and collect information about HIV/Aids. Encourage discussion at school and provide new information whenever possible. Guide learners to feel empathy for people living with HIV/Aids.

- Use some of the poems as inspiration for the learners to write their own poems.

- Discuss the importance of being optimistic about the future. Ask learners to find letters in which Madiba's positive attitude is evident, and to decide how they can use his example in their own lives. Learners can identify problems at school or in the community and look for positive ways to approach these problems.

- The letter on page 38 mentions the power of the child. Read and discuss the rights of children, according to the Constitution. Make sure learners understand the links between rights and responsibilities.

Using *Letters to Madiba* at school with learners in Grade 7

- Let learners work in groups to discuss and suggest practical ways to solve problems such as crime, poverty and drug abuse.

- Some other famous South Africans are mentioned on pages 46 and 87. Learners can do research on these people and on famous musicians, politicians, leaders, writers, actors and sports people.

- The writer of the letter on page 87 discusses the changing role of women in South Africa. Ask learners to think of practical ways in which they, as adolescents, can make a conscious effort to think and behave differently in order to change the role and perceptions of women.

- A few letters mention the Nelson Mandela Children's Fund. Others tell Madiba what they need. In groups, learners can decide on a charity they would like to support and they can list ways they could raise funds for this charity.

- Many of the letters provide the opportunity to discuss tourism. Discuss topics like why tourists enjoy visiting a country, things that discourage them from visiting a country, tourist attractions in your region, tourists and the economy and so on. Learners can do a research project and make brochures, write advertisements, design posters and think of ideas for entrepreneurial activities about tourism.

Enjoy reading and using the letters both as a resource and a source of inspiration, insight and positive thought.

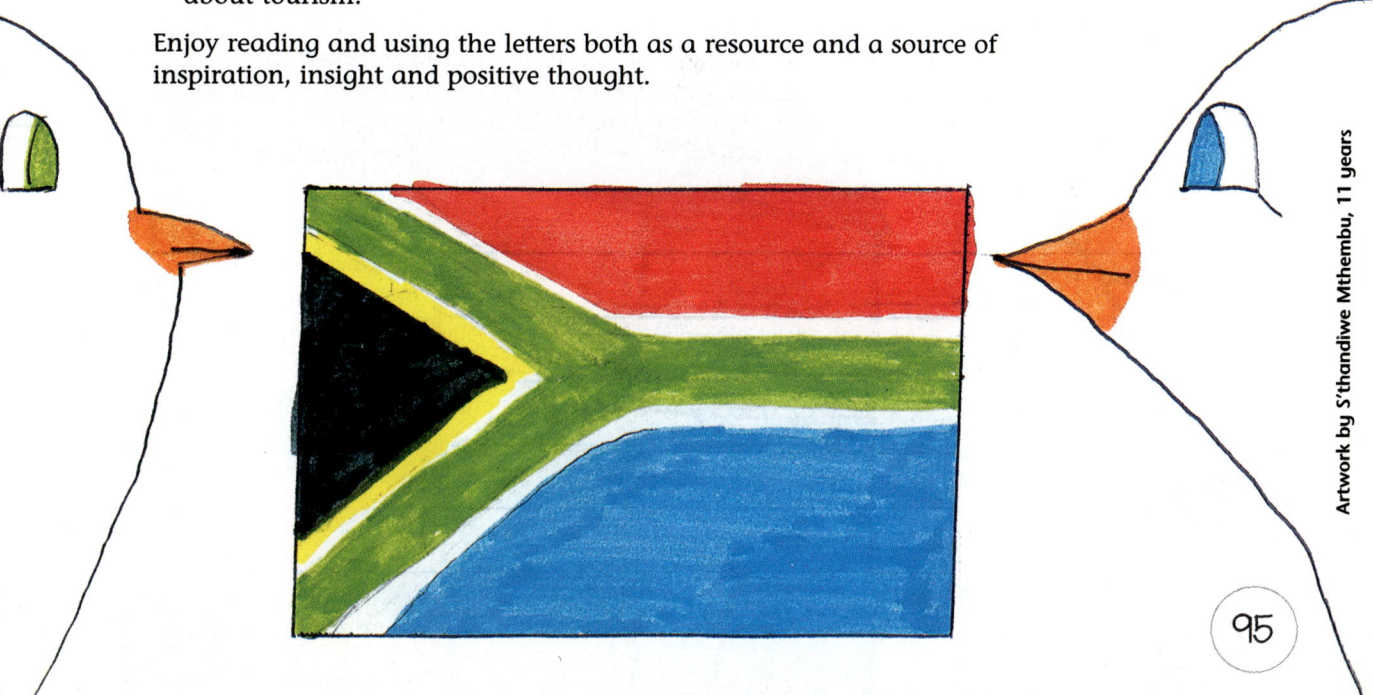

Artwork by S'thandiwe Mthembu, 11 years

Maskew Miller Longman (Pty) Ltd
Forest Drive, Pinelands, Cape Town

Offices in Johannesburg, Durban, King William's Town, Pietersburg, Bloemfontein, representatives in Mafikeng and companies throughout southern and central Africa.

website: www.mml.co.za

© Maskew Miller Longman (Pty) Ltd 2002

All rights reserved. No part of this publication may be reproduced, stored in a retrieval system, or transmitted in any form or by any means, electronic, mechanical, photocopying, recording, or otherwise, without the prior written permission of the copyright holder.

First published in 2002

ISBN 0 636 04973 6

The series editor is Lesley Beake
Edited by Clarice Smuts
Book design by Elize Schultz
Cover artwork by Lebogo Mokatse, Choki Lubabalo Nxele Mabi, Martin Mambolo, Nowellen Hartnick, Sheree O'Donoghue, Sithembiso Mqadi, Doro Piliswa and Karen Govender
Cover design by Amaal Bruwer
Cover photograph by Andy Katz (*Business Day*)
Title page photograph by John Haigh
Artwork by South African children
Scanning and reproduction by Castle Graphics and Hirt and Carter

Printed by CTP Book Printers

Although every attempt was made to identify each letter-writer and young artist this could not be done in some cases.

Artwork by Balingile, Grade 1